Economically Developing Countries

South Korea

Sung-Hoon Jung

RSVP
RAINTREE
STECK-VAUGHN
P U B L I S H E R S
The Steck-Vaughn Company

Austin, Texas

Economically Developing Countries

Bangladesh	**Malaysia**
Brazil	**Mexico**
China	**Nigeria**
Egypt	**Peru**
Ghana	**South Korea**
India	**Vietnam**

Cover: A market trader holding ginseng roots, a valuable plant that has medicinal qualities
Title page: The South Korea World Trade Center in Seoul
Contents page: Taekwondo, the national sport, is now popular in many other countries.

Picture acknowledgments:

Action-Plus *Contents Page*; Axiom/Jim Holmes 6, 9 (bottom), 10 (bottom), 18, 19, 20, 21, 22, 23, 24, 25, 27 (bottom), 28 (top), 29 (top), 30, 31, 32 (bottom), 34, 36, 37, 38, 39 (right), 41, 42 (bottom), 43 (top), 44 (top), 45 (top); Hulton Deutsch 8, 9 (top); Image Bank *Cover* (Kevin Forest); Popperfoto 7, 10 (top), 11, 45 (bottom). The publishers would also like to thank the Korea National Tourism Organization and the Embassy of the Republic of Korea for providing the remaining photographs used in this book. All maps are by Peter Bull.

Published by Raintree Steck-Vaughn Publishers, an imprint of Steck-Vaughn Company

Library of Congress Cataloging-in-Publication Data
Jung, Sung-Hoon.
South Korea / Sung-Hoon Jung.
    p.   cm.—(Economically developing countries)
    Includes bibliographical references and index.
    Summary: Explores the recent history, geography, current economy, and future of South Korea
    ISBN 0-8172-4530-8
    1. Korea (South)—Juvenile literature.
    [1. Korea (South).]
    I. Title. II. Series.
    DS902.J88 1997
    951.95—dc20   96-17969

Printed in Italy. Bound in the United States.
1 2 3 4 5 6 7 8 9 0 01 00 99 98 97

Contents

Introduction

South Korea lies on the southern half of the Korean peninsula, in East Asia. To the north are North Korea and China, to the northeast lies Russia, and to the southeast are the islands of Japan. A distance of only 118 miles to China and 112 miles to the Japanese island of Honshu has led to various political, economic, and cultural links among South Korea and its neighbors.

South Korea is one of a number of countries that have experienced rapid economic growth since World War II. Today, most South Koreans are enjoying this wealth. However, behind the country's fast economic growth lie many historical and political difficulties.

"(Historically) sandwiched between vastly more powerful neighbors (especially China and Japan), who, for at least two millennia, have sought to absorb it, South Korea has nevertheless preserved its own unique character and cultural identity."—from **Korea by Robert Storey and Geoff Crowther (Lonely Planet Publications, 1995)**

GROWING ASIAN ECONOMIES			
Country	Population (million)	GNP (billion $)	Growth rate (%) (1985–93)
Japan	125	3,924	3.6
China	1,175	581	6.5
Hong Kong	6	105	5.3
South Korea	44	338	8.1
Indonesia	187	137	4.8
Singapore	3	55	6.1

Source: *The European Union and Asia* (European Commission, 1995)

The traditional fan dance of Korea. Korean culture has survived many changes in the twentieth century.

4

Left South Korea is a mountainous country. This is Mt. Sanbang on Cheju Island.

SOUTH KOREA AT A GLANCE

Capital:	Seoul
Population:	44,553,880 (annual rate of increase: 0.9%)
Currency:	Won (W)
Area:	38,330 sq. mi.
Total coastline:	10,750 miles
Highest mountain:	Mt. Halla (6,400 feet), on Cheju Island
Largest island:	Cheju (705 sq. mi.)

Source: *Korea Annual* (Yonhap News Agency, 1995)

— Major roads
┅┅┅ Railroads
✈ International airport
✈ Airport to be completed in 2000

On August 15, 1945, independence was restored to Korea, as thirty-six years of Japanese rule over the nation came to an end. Korean people marched down the streets in celebration. However, just five years later, on June 25, 1950, a war broke out between the southern and northern parts of Korea. The war was to last for three years. An armistice agreement was signed between the two sides on July 27, 1953, but since then Korea has been divided into South Korea and North Korea.

5

The South Korean flag, called *Taegukki*, symbolizes peace, unity, creation, brightness, and infinity. The red half of the central circle represents the *Yang*, meaning heaven, day, male, and heat; the blue half symbolizes the *Um*, which means earth, night, female, and cold. In oriental philosophy, these two opposites represent the balance and harmony of the universe.

The three lines at each corner also have opposite meanings. The three parallel, unbroken bars on the upper left-hand corner represent heaven, while opposite them the three broken bars represent earth. The bars in the upper right corner represent the moon, and those in the lower left corner represent the sun.

The white background symbolizes purity, or the Buddhist idea of emptiness.

A flag similar to this one was created in 1882. The current design became the national flag in 1948.

Above Taegukki, *the national flag of South Korea*

Below *Electronic goods in a Seoul store*

Over the last forty years, South Korea has enjoyed economic growth and, together with Hong Kong, Singapore, and Taiwan, it has become one of the nations known as the "Asian tigers." Since the 1970s, South Korea has had an annual economic growth rate between 8 and 9 percent. In 1995, the country was the fourth biggest exporter of electronic goods in the world. It was also the third biggest producer of semi-conductors, after the United States and Japan.

Modern History

During the late nineteenth and early twentieth centuries, Japan, China, and Russia fought for control of Korea. The struggles began when, in 1894, large *Tonghak* demonstrations by Korean farmers spread rapidly throughout the country. *Tonghak* was an eastern philosophy that made Korean farmers more conscious of their poor living conditions and caused them to rebel against their government. The central government was so weak that it was unable to fight against the farmers, so it asked China for military aid. However, China tried to gain a permanent influence over Korea, and this caused Japan to declare war on China in Korea, in 1894.

After the defeat of China, Japan controlled the government of Korea in the city of Seoul. Shortly after this, however, Russia tried to take control of Korea, which led to war between Russia and Japan in Korea in 1904. After Russia's defeat, Korea was occupied by the Japanese.

Two Koreans put their votes into a ballot box, in the first democratic elections of the newly created Republic of South Korea, in 1948.

JAPANESE RULE (1910–1945)

In 1910, Japanese rule over Korea began and was to last for thirty-six years. To the Korean people, this era was a dark age, like the Middle Ages in Europe, because they lost everything, including their own language, culture, and natural resources. Despite continuous resistance against Japan, liberation was not easy to achieve. Freedom came only with Japan's surrender at the end of World War II, in August 1945.

7

THE KOREAN WAR (1950–53)

Three years after its liberation from Japan in 1945, Korea put itself under the protection of the United States and the U.S.S.R. The United States occupied the southern part of Korea and the U.S.S.R. occupied the north, above the 38th parallel. During this period, when Korea suffered its second "dark age," as the clash between two different types of government—the capitalism of the United States and the communism of the U.S.S.R.—caused conflict and tension.

At 4:00 A.M. on June 25, 1950, the Korean War suddenly broke out with North Korea's invasion of the south. In the early stages of the war, North Korea occupied almost the whole of South Korea, and South Korea urgently called for help from other countries. Some 16 countries, including the United States and Great Britain, acting under the name of the United Nations (UN), came to help South Korea.

"The Korean War of 1950–53 was the most important war ever fought between the West and communism. It saw sixteen armies…deployed under U.S. command and the UN flag, against two armies, those of North Korea and China. It brought the people of Korea appalling destruction, devastation, and tragedy; there were millions of deaths and more millions of divided families. Yet it is still an unknown war, with unraveled mysteries…."—From **Korea: The Unknown War** *by Jon Halliday and Bruce Cumings (Viking, 1988)*

South Korean troops on patrol in the bombed town of Pohang in 1950. The ruins of the bombed town provided ideal cover for North Korean snipers.

8

South Korean and UN forces regained South Korea, and then started to invade the north. After just a month of fighting, North Korea requested help from the U.S.S.R. and China. The Chinese government added an enormous military force to the war and with the North Koreans recovered the territory of North Korea. On July 27, 1953, hostilities were finally called off, and an armistice agreement was signed between North and South Korea. The pact has been in place ever since.

During the last forty years, the South Korean government has developed new foreign policies to reflect changing international relations, such as the end of the Cold War. Now the former U.S.S.R., China, and even Japan are no longer hostile to South Korea. However, the tension and conflict between South and North Korea remains.

__Above__ South Korean soldiers on their way to the battlefront

__Below__ A surveillance camera watches over the border between South and North Korea

SOUTH KOREA SINCE 1953

After the end of the Korean War, the South Korean economy was slow in recovering, and the government was weak. One person who was dissatisfied with the government was General Chung-Hee Park. In May 1961, Park led a military revolution against the government, at the head of his own army.

Park established a military dictatorship and in 1963 became president. He had a strong influence on the rapid economic growth of South Korea, particularly through his powerful personality and leadership. His government constantly intervened in the country's economy, which could be described at this time as a state-oriented economy.

Above *After ruling as a military dictator, Park was elected president in 1963.*

CHANGING GNP PER CAPITA OF SOUTH KOREA						
	1973	1975	1980	1985	1990	1993
GNP per capita ($)	430	640	1,053	2,260	5,770	7,660

Source: World Bank, 1995

Right *The growth of heavy industry was an important feature of the state-oriented economy from the 1970s to the 1980s.*

Under Park, the human and natural resources of the nation were well organized for the first time in the twentieth century. The economy started to grow at an annual rate of 9.2 percent. Gross National Product (GNP) per person rose from $87 in 1962 to $1,503 in 1980, and exports increased dramatically in the same period, from $56.7 million in 1962 to $17.5 billion in 1980. However, during Park's presidency, democracy and human rights suffered.

Park remained in power for eighteen years, until, on October 26, 1979, he was assassinated by one of his followers, Chae-Kyu Kim, the chief of the Korean Central Intelligence Agency. Between 1980 and 1993 two presidents were elected who came from the army, and military dictatorship continued. Finally, in 1993, the first civilian leader, President Young-Sam Kim, was elected in South Korea, after thirty-two years of military rule.

South Korea's first civilian president, Young-Sam Kim (left), takes over from Tae-Woo Roh.

KEY DATES OF MODERN SOUTH KOREA

1894	Tonghak revolution.
	Sino-Japanese War is won by the Japanese.
1904–5	Russo-Japanese War. Japan conquers Korea.
1910	Japanese rule over Korea begins.
1919	March 1—Korean Independence Movement begins against Japan.
1945	Liberation of Korea from Japanese rule.
1948	Republic of Korea (South Korea) created.
1948	Elections: Dr. Syngman Rhee becomes president of South Korea.
1950	June 25—The Korean War breaks out between South and North Korea.
1953	Armistice between South and North Korea.
1961	Military coup led by General Chung-Hee Park.
1966	The South Korean government sends 45,000 troops to fight for South Vietnam.
1979	President Park is assassinated.
1980	Doo Huan Chun is chosen as president.
1987	Tae-Woo Roh is elected president.
1988	Olympic Games are held in Seoul.
1991	South Korea joins UN.
1993	The Young-Sam Kim administration begins.

Land and Climate

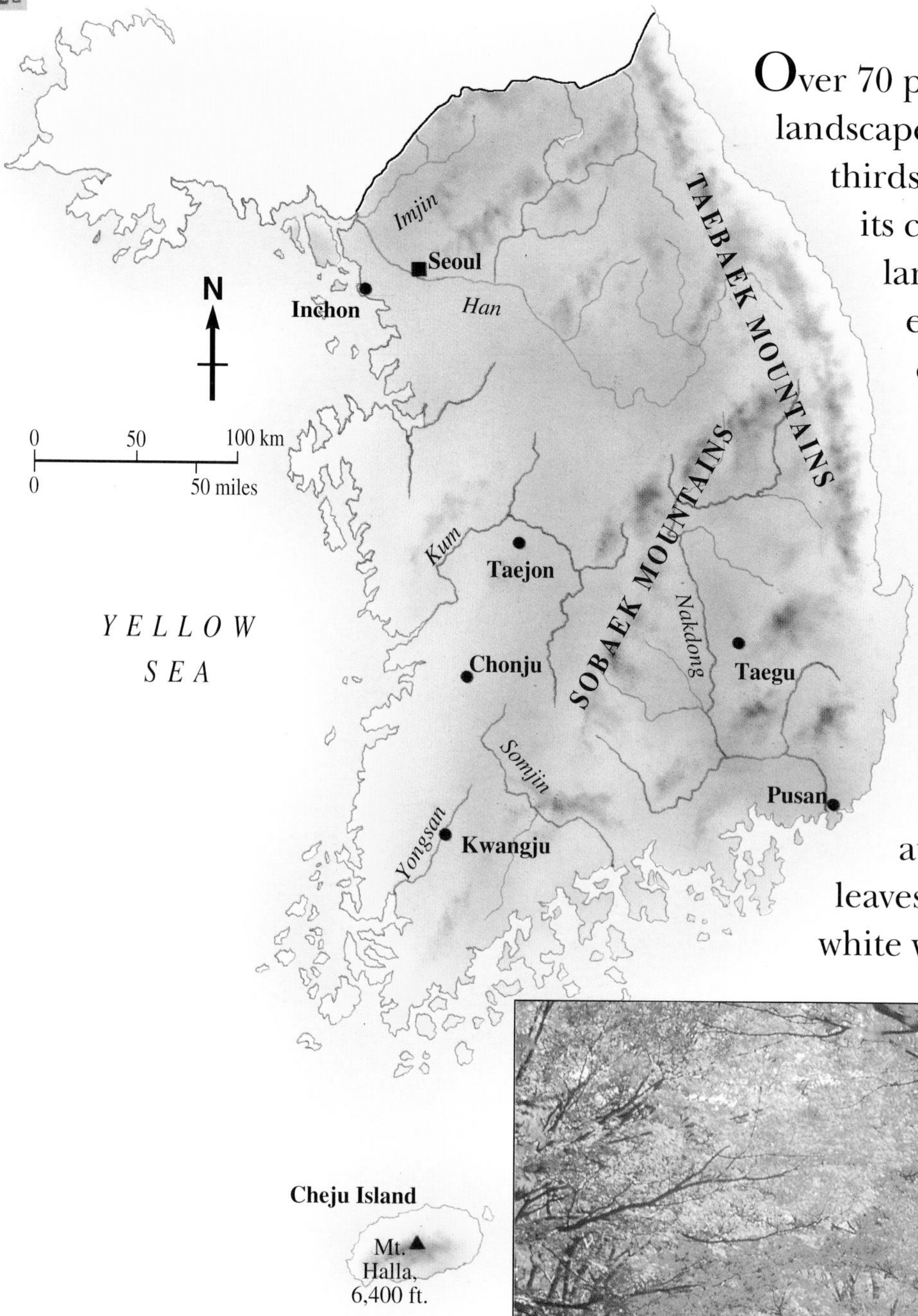

Over 70 percent of the South Korean landscape is mountainous, and two thirds is covered by forests. Despite its closeness to Japan, Korean land is stable and does not experience the powerful earthquakes of Japan. The Taebaek mountain range forms the "backbone" of the country. Each season, these mountains take on a new color. In spring, they turn yellow, as new leaves appear on the trees; in summer, grasses and flowers turn them green and blue; in autumn, they glow with red leaves; and in winter, they become white with snow.

YELLOW SEA

TAEBAEK MOUNTAINS

SOBAEK MOUNTAINS

Imjin
Seoul
Inchon
Han
Kum
Taejon
Chonju
Nakdong
Taegu
Somjin
Pusan
Yongsan
Kwangju

Cheju Island
Mt. Halla, 6,400 ft.

The country around Mt. Naejang, in the southwest, is famous for its autumn colors.

12

Above In the southeast of the country, there is a spectacular rocky landscape near the coast.

Below Seoul has developed along the banks of the Han River.

RIVERS

The shape of the land causes most of South Korea's rivers to flow from the northern and eastern areas into the Yellow Sea to the west or into the Sea of Japan to the south. Whereas most of South Korea's mountains are located in the northern and eastern areas, most rivers are in the western and southern regions. The rivers are mostly short, shallow, and fast flowing. They have played an important role in the social, political, and economic life of the country.

The capital city, Seoul, for example, developed beside the Han River, which provided an important transportation route. After the introduction of a modern system of roads and railroads, the rivers became less important for transportation, but they still contribute extensively to the irrigation of rice fields, as they have done for many centuries. At present, about 12 percent of rice fields rely upon rivers for irrigation.

13

The rivers are surrounded by beautiful landscapes. The source of the Han River is in the northeast of South Korea, and it flows through Seoul to the northwest coast. In the mountainous landscape of the northeast, the Han supplies hydroelectric power (HEP) stations. In Seoul, urban development has taken place along the river. The southern branch of the Han is a tourist attraction and there, too, the river powers an HEP station.

COASTLINES AND ISLANDS

There are about 3,000 islands off the south and southwest coasts of South Korea. The east coast has a smooth outline, whereas the south and the west coasts are complex, with many islands, small peninsulas, and bays. The landscapes of the coastline and islands are stunning.

Above *Dawn on the Han River. The southern branch of the river flows through the beautiful Todam Sambong Park.*

Below *Seagulls hover above fishing boats near Hong Island, off the southwest coast.*

Cheju Island

Left *The Chungmun resort on Cheju. The island is popular with South Korean and foreign tourists.*

in South Korea, at 6,400 feet, and it has about 360 volcanic cones. The landscape of Cheju Island is completely different from that of the mainland, and the language, culture, and lifestyle are quite exotic. Many South Koreans from the mainland, together with foreign tourists, enjoy their vacations on the island.

Cheju Island, the largest in South Korea, is particularly beautiful. The island had a record of minor volcanic activity from A.D. 918–1392, so it has many volcanic landforms. One mountain on the island, Mount Halla, is the highest

LAND USE
Only 30 percent of South Korea's land area is flat, and the population is concentrated on these plains. Since the 1960s, industrial land use has sharply increased, whereas agricultural land use has dramatically decreased. This is a result of rapid industrialization and urbanization. The change in the pattern of land use means that South Korean society has been transformed from a combination of agricultural and rural to an industrial and urban society.

Above *Orange trees on Cheju Island, with Mt. Halla, South Korea's highest mountain, in the distance.*

CLIMATE

There are four seasons a year in South Korea. In general, the climate is humid and east-Asian monsoonal. Spring is rather short—usually less than three months, lasting from March to the end of May. To South Korean people, spring means the start of everything, because as the weather gets warmer, people begin to work more actively. Summer is quite hot, with temperatures sometimes above 86°F. This is also the season of cyclonic storms and monsoonal rains. July, in particular, has heavy rain that causes floods, and thousands of people are often made homeless. However, abundant rainfall and hot summers are necessary for growing rice. Autumn in South Korea is very pleasant, but rather short, like the spring. The weather is cool, and the sky is blue and clear. Winter is quite cold, with snow and average temperatures generally below freezing. The average temperature in January in Seoul is 26°F.

Above Walkers cross the bridge on Mt. Taedun, in central South Korea. Winters in South Korea are cold with temperatures often below freezing.

Opposite Cherry trees in bloom in Chinhae, during the short spring season

16

SOUTH KOREA'S CLIMATE

Average January temperatures
- above 36°F
- 32° to 36°F
- 25° to 32°F
- 18° to 25°F

Average August temperatures
- 79°F
- 77°F
- 75°F
- 72° to 75°F

Average precipitation, Dec.–Feb.
- above 7 inches
- 5–7 inches
- 3–5 inches
- 1–3 inches

Average precipitation, June–August
- 28–32 inches
- 24–28 inches
- 20–24 inches
- 16–20 inches

The Economy— An "Asian Tiger"

The South Korean government has described the country's economic performance over the last forty years as "compressed growth," meaning rapid growth over a short period of time.

THE SOUTH KOREAN ECONOMY	
GNP (1994):	$376.9 billion
GNP per capita (1994):	$8,483
Exports (1993):	$82.3 billion
Imports (1993):	$81.3 billion

SOUTH KOREAN INDUSTRIALIZATION

Since the late 1960s, South Korea, traditionally a typical agricultural country, has changed dramatically into an industrialized country. Industry, especially manufacturing, has played an important role in economic growth. South Korean industrialization is based on the export of manufactured goods rather than on raw materials, because the country has no natural resources such as oil, natural gas, or minerals. There have been three distinct stages of industrialization: light, heavy, and high-tech. Each of these stages has involved the development of different industrial regions.

Many light industries can be found in the export-processing zone in Kuro Dong, Seoul.

During the 1960s and up to the mid-1970s, the South Korean industrial economy was dominated by light industries, which produced and exported goods such as textiles, clothing, and footwear. These light industries needed plenty of cheap labor. Several light-industrial complexes, called free export zones, grew up near urban areas. Here there was a ready supply of workers, especially women, who were willing to accept low wages.

Between the mid-1970s and mid-1980s, South Korea tried to increase the number of its heavy industries, such as shipbuilding and automobile, chemical, and steel manufacturing. These industries needed huge amounts of money and equipment, as well as plenty of cheap but qualified labor. The heavy-industrial zones of South Korea developed on the southeastern coasts, especially near ports, which provided good facilities for exporting goods.

A skilled worker uses machinery at a shipyard in Ulsan, a city on the southeast coast.

"How can a country where the working week is thirty or thirty-five hours compete with South Korea?"(The average South Korean working week is forty-five to forty-eight hours.)—*from* **Towards a New Economic Order b y Alain Lipietz (Polity, 1992)**

MAJOR INDUSTRIES

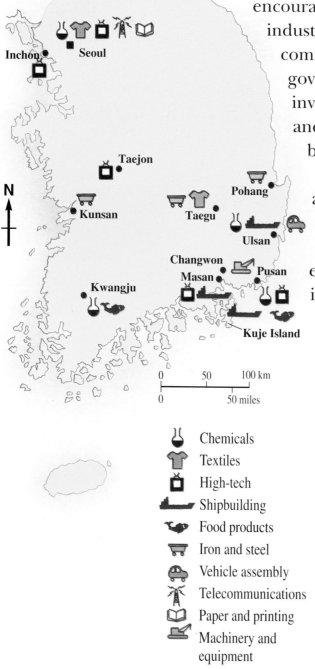

Since the mid-1980s, South Korea has been encouraging the transition from heavy to high-tech industries, such as the computer, semiconductor, communication, and media industries. The government and private companies have invested much money in these industries, and several high-tech industrial sites have been established near large cities.

Despite these dynamic manufacturing activities, service industries have gradually increased in the 1990s, while manufacturing has slightly decreased. The South Korean economy may be dominated by service industries in the future.

Chemicals
Textiles
High-tech
Shipbuilding
Food products
Iron and steel
Vehicle assembly
Telecommunications
Paper and printing
Machinery and equipment

Above *Technological development and fast economic growth have led to new jobs in service industries. Here, a tourist office worker uses computer information networks.*

INDUSTRIAL SECTOR'S SHARE OF GROSS DOMESTIC PRODUCT (%)						
	1966	1971	1976	1981	1986	1992
Tertiary	44.7	51	48.1	53.1	55.9	64.7
Secondary	20.5	23.2	28.4	31.3	32.6	27.7
Primary	34.8	26.8	23.5	15.6	11.5	7.6

Source: The Bank of Korea (1993)

TRADE

Since South Korea has no natural resources, the economy has to depend on "processing trade," that is, the importing and processing of raw materials and the exporting of them as finished goods. The type of goods exported has varied, according to each stage of South Korea's industrialization. In the 1970s, South Korean goods in stores throughout the world were mainly clothing and footwear. Since the 1980s, however, South Korean exports have reflected the country's major investments in the shipbuilding, car manufacturing, and electronics industries. South Korea's main trade partners since the 1960s have been the United States and Japan.

EXPORT AND IMPORT PARTNERS (1992)

	Exports (%)	Imports (%)
U.S.	23.6	22.4
Japan	15.1	23.8
Hong Kong	7.7	1.0
Germany	3.8	4.6
Taiwan	3.0	1.6
Indonesia	2.5	2.8
UK	2.4	1.7
Others	41.9	42.1

Source: *A Handbook of Korea* (Korean Overseas Information Service, 1993)

THE TRANSPORTATION SYSTEM

South Korea has one of the world's best public transportation systems, including buses, trains, boats, and planes. The first railroad was built at the beginning of the twentieth century, and during Japanese rule a rough railroad network was established to link major cities. After the Korean War, most railroads had to be rebuilt.

Express trains run between many important cities.

The Seoul subway system is fast and extensive and is one solution to the problem of city traffic jams.

Since the 1960s, the government has been developing a national network of highways. The first highway, between Seoul and Inchon, was constructed in 1968, and the second, between Seoul and Pusan, in 1970. Since then, networks of highways and railroads between cities, and underground railroads within cities, have been established. At present, an expensive high-speed rail link is being built between Seoul and Pusan, in technological cooperation with France.

The transportation system of South Korea has influenced the location of new industrial developments and has led to an unequal pattern of development. For example, since the 1970s, the highway between Seoul and Pusan has created a corridor of concentrated growth between the two cities.

CHAEBOLS

One of the most important factors in the economic growth of South Korea has been the growth of *chaebols*—conglomerates, or family businesses—such as Samsung and Hyundai. In 1987, *chaebols* provided 17.6 percent of the employment and produced 37.3 percent of the total output of the South Korean economy. Since the government supports the growth of *chaebols*, the South Korean economy is said to be state- and *chaebol*-oriented.

There are between thirty and fifty *chaebols* in South Korea. Some say that if one of the *chaebols* collapsed, the country would face a considerable economic crisis, which indicates how dependent the economy is on these family businesses. One of the problems of *chaebols*, however, is that they invest in similar industries and then compete with one another in domestic and world markets.

The road network has been developed and improved, but traffic jams are now a major problem.

CHAEBOLS AND THE KOREAN ECONOMY			
	1977	1982	1987
Share of total employment	20.5	18.6	17.6
Share of total output	34.1	40.7	37.3

Source: *Chaebols and economic concentration*, G. U. Lee (Korea Development Institute, 1990)

Samsung and Hyundai— International Successes

Samsung and Hyundai are two successful *chaebols*. Samsung is famous for electronic goods such as televisions, cameras, and semiconductors, which are sold all over the world. Hyundai is famous for heavy goods such as cars, ships, and construction equipment.

The founder of Samsung was the late Byung-Chull Lee, who ran a rice-cleaning mill during the period of Japanese rule. After the Korean War, Lee became interested in manufacturing, especially in the refined sugar and woolen textile industries. These industries were the basis of Samsung's growth. In the 1960s, Samsung concentrated on general wholesale and retail, aimed at the world market. In this period, the South Korean government put an

Right *A television set on a Samsung production line*

Left *Doo Yeol Choi*

*"In the last twenty years everything seems to have changed in Korea, but the greatest moves have been made in industry and technology. The whole multimedia market has been created; it really is a world without frontiers. I'm proud of what we have achieved at Samsung Electronics, and in Korean industry in general, because years ago we had so many problems, but now we can compete shoulder-to-shoulder with other international companies."—**Doo Yeol Choi, manager at Samsung Electronics**

export-oriented economic policy into practice. In the 1970s, Samsung invested heavily in the electronics, shipbuilding, chemical, and construction industries. In the 1980s, the company developed several semiconductors and later exported goods such as video recorders, televisions, and cameras. Today, Samsung is one of the biggest companies not only in South Korea, but also throughout the world.

The founder of Hyundai was Chu-Young Chung, who was an assistant in a rice shop during Japanese rule. He then managed a rice shop and later ran a garage. During the Korean War, Chung was involved in construction work and had close relations with the U.S. Army in South Korea. After the war, Hyundai became involved in construction work in several countries besides South Korea. The company also invested in the automobile and shipbuilding industries.

In the late 1960s, Hyundai formed a contract with Ford, one of the most famous companies in the United States, and set up an auto assembly plant in Ulsan, in southeastern Korea. In 1973, the company started to produce cars, using its own technology. In the 1980s, Hyundai turned to the electronics industry, producing semiconductors, computers, and communication equipment. Like Samsung, Hyundai is now one of the biggest companies in the world.

Hyundai's shipyard in Ulsan, a city that has grown with the company

People and Society

The rapid growth of their economy has meant that South Koreans are caught between traditional and modern lifestyles. For example, fast-food restaurants are common sights on the city streets. So what is the traditional culture of South Korea? And how is it being modernized?

THE FAMILY

South Korea was traditionally a Confucian society, one in which family values were based on the ancient teachings of the Chinese philosopher Confucius. The typical Korean family was large, with several generations living together under one roof. The head of the family was regarded as the figure of authority, and all family members were expected to obey the family head. It would have been unthinkable for children or grandchildren to act against their elders' wishes.

A South Korean bride in colorful traditional dress

THE SOUTH KOREAN POPULATION	
Life expectancy (1993):	72.2 years
Birth rate (1991):	15.6 per 1,000
Mortality rate (1991):	5.8 per 1,000
Child mortality rate (0–4 years, 1991):	12.8 per 1,000
Population per doctor (1993):	855
Literacy (1987):	99%

Source: *A Handbook of Korea* (Korean Overseas Information Service, 1993)

26

Left *The New Year's Day greeting is traditionally offered to older relatives. Here, children greet their grandparents.*

Below *Jung Hwan Seo, a retired 66-year-old South Korean*

However, over the last thirty years, the urbanization of South Korea has meant that two-generation, or "nuclear" families, are increasing, because city homes are usually only large enough for two generations. Since the 1970s, young people have had different lifestyles from those of their ancestors. They prefer Westernized lifestyles and do not respect their elders as much. Even though many customs of a Confucian society remain, elderly South Koreans are worried that their traditional culture is being destroyed.

"When I was young, life was so hard we shared the little we had and hoped the situation would get better. Hard work and good ideas have brought Korea into the modern world. Now, of course, young people don't know what real struggle is like; they have everything they want—they spend their money on new clothes, foreign food, and vacations abroad, when they should be thinking of the future."
—Jung Hwan Seo, age 66, retired

RELIGIONS

Throughout the twentieth century, the number of people in South Korea following the traditional beliefs of Confucianism and Buddhism has declined, whereas Protestantism and Catholicism have become more popular. Most Buddhist temples are located high up in the mountains, whereas Protestant and Catholic churches are in the city streets.

RELIGIONS IN SOUTH KOREA, 1991	
Buddhism:	51.2%
Protestantism:	34.4%
Catholicism:	10.6%
Confucianism:	1.8%
Others:	2.0%

Source: *A Handbook of Korea* (Korean Overseas Information Service, 1993)

Above *This modern church in Seoul —claimed to be the world's largest— reflects the growing importance of Christianity.*

Left *Pulguk Temple, in Kyongju, is Korea's best-known Buddhist temple.*

Weddings and Funerals

In the Confucian tradition, partners for marriage were chosen by the parents of the bride or bridegroom, rather than by the young people themselves. The parents arranged the marriage with the help of a fortune-teller, in a process called the *Kung-hap*. The result of the *Kung-hap* was important because it suggested whether the young couple could live together happily. If the *Kung-hap* was bad, the marriage would be canceled. Traditional wedding ceremonies were usually held at the bride's house. The ceremony began with the bride and groom exchanging bows and drinks, facing each other over the wedding table. Today the *Kung-hap* is not as important, and modern wedding ceremonies are more similar to Western weddings than to those of the Korean tradition.

Above *A Western-style wedding*
Left *the traditional wedding ceremony*

In the past, it was very important for people to die in their own homes, surrounded by their families. In the traditional Confucian style, the coffin was carried to the grave in a great procession. Leading the procession were people carrying funeral flags and burning incense, and there was usually someone ringing a bell and singing in a deep, mournful voice. Now most people, especially in cities, die in hospitals, and the funeral service reflects the religion of the deceased.

Carrying the coffin to the grave in a traditional procession

A Long Day

Many South Koreans believe that children suffer because their day is as long as most adults' working day.

Ho-Jung Lim is eleven years old and attends primary school. She goes to school from Monday to Saturday, six days a week. Ho-Jung's day is typical of other South Korean schoolchildren's. On school days, Ho-Jung gets up at 7:00 A.M. and is at school by 8.30 A.M. She gets home from school about 3:00 P.M. and then has to be at an art class by 4:00 P.M. After the art lesson, which lasts for one and a half hours, Ho-Jung goes home again. At 6:00 P.M., she goes to an English language center for a one-hour lesson in English. After that, she has to take a music lesson for an hour. At 8:30 P.M., Ho-Jung goes home and then has to do homework for her school and other studies. She goes to bed between 10:00 and 11:00 P.M.

"If my daughter is to become a good person, whom we and society want, she needs this variety of education from birth."
—Soo Bong Lim, Ho-Jung's father

EDUCATION

Education is extremely important to South Korean parents. Literacy has sharply increased, from 22 percent in 1953 to 89 percent in 1970 and to 99 percent in 1987. South Korean parents always spend considerable amounts of money on their children's education.

Children in South Korea start school at six years old and go to primary school until they are eleven. From primary school they go to middle school, from twelve to fourteen years, and then on to high school, until the age of seventeen.

Children at work in a primary school in Seoul

30

For most South Korean people, one of the most important things for both adults and children is to learn English. The ability to speak English affects a person's chances of entering a good university and succeeding in business. There are many English colleges in South Korea with teachers from countries whose native language is English. They offer courses for children and adults at every level. These colleges are popular because most South Korean people prefer to learn English from native English teachers rather than from South Koreans.

Above The ability to speak English is very important to South Koreans. Adults as well as children take language lessons.

"My two children go to private English language school here in Seoul. I grew up in the twentieth century but my children will live in the twenty-first century, and I'm sure English will be the world language of the next century. This knowledge will help them to compete for jobs and a good life as they grow up."

—*Pong Hewi Kim, mother of Hang Ju Lee, 8, and Hong Ju Lee, 10 years old*

Above Pong Hewi Kim with her children

After high school, students can attend junior college, college, and a university, for between two and four years. In order to enter a good university, students face fierce competition in entrance examinations. It is important to attend a good university because the universities are graded, and the grade of a university influences the types of jobs offered to its students. Most people in South Korea call this strong competition "the evil of the entrance examination."

WOMEN

In traditional South Korean society, women's activities were limited to the home. They were expected to follow the Confucian virtues of respect for authority and patience and to support their husbands and children at home. However, with the industrialization of South Korea, the role and status of women have changed. Since the 1960s, young women in their early twenties have supplied cheap labor to factories and have thus contributed to the nation's economic growth. Recently, however, the largest increase in employment for women has been in the service sector.

"The women of Korea are trying hard to meet the changes in our society. Roles are changing here, and all women need is the opportunity to compete on an equal basis to prove their value in many professional fields. As more women go through higher education and gain specialized knowledge, this situation will change more rapidly. But there is some distance to go yet, and women still have to work harder than men to compete on the same level."
– Dr. Seok Ran Shim, educational director of school

Above *Traditional clothes are still often worn on special occasions such as weddings and festivals.*

Right *Dr. Seok Ran Shim*

32

LEISURE AND SPORTS

As South Koreans have become wealthier, leisure activities have increased. This has meant that various new leisure facilities, such as golf courses and ski resorts, have been developed. People take vacations at different locations, depending on the season. In the winter, many people go skiing in mountain resorts; in the summer beaches are popular. Above all, most South Korean people enjoy watching soccer and baseball on weekends, from spring until autumn. Skiing and golf are becoming more popular, because they are set in beautiful surroundings.

Below (inset)
Muju ski resort in the southwest is the largest in South Korea.

Below Many South Koreans enjoy watching and playing baseball.

In the Cities

The rapid economic growth and industrialization of South Korea have caused a process of intense city growth since the 1960s. In particular, large cities such as Seoul and Pusan have spread outward. Urban growth has caused a decline in the population of rural areas and has led to severe traffic jams, environmental pollution, and an increase in inner-city crime.

Below *Like most modern cities, South Korean cities are affected by pollution from industry and heavy traffic.*

URBANIZATION COMPARED TO INDUSTRIALIZATION, 1960–90		
	Rate of urbanization (%)	Rate of industrialization (%)
1960	35.5	34.1
1970	49.8	49.6
1980	68.7	66.0
1990	82.8	81.7

Source: *Economic development and the change of spatial structure in Korea*, D. H. Kim (1992)

Above Expo Park, where Taejon Expo '93 was held. Taejon is becoming a major scientific center.

After the Korean War, huge numbers of people migrated from the countryside to Seoul and Pusan. Many were attracted to the cities because they believed they could find jobs there. Today, it is said that everything from South Korea is concentrated in Seoul. The capital city's population accounts for about a quarter of the total population of South Korea.

However, present-day Seoul faces serious urban problems, such as heavy traffic that causes jams, and pollution, as a result of its large population. Land is expensive, and there is a shortage of land for housing. Other large cities, such as Pusan, Taejon, and Kwangju, have challenged the status of Seoul with their own growth and have successfully attracted national and international organizations to major cultural events.

CITY POPULATIONS (1990)	
Seoul:	10,612,577
Pusan:	3,798,113
Taegu:	2,229,040
Inchon:	1,817,919
Kwangju:	1,139,003
Taejon:	1,049,578
Source: *The Europa World Year Book* (1994)	

35

VIEWS OF SEOUL

Seoul is about 600 years old and dates back to the beginning of the Yi dynasty, which lasted from A.D. 1392 to A.D. 1910. The city is the political, economic, and educational center of the country. Industrialization and urbanization have modernized the landscape, totally changing the city's appearance. Old palaces have been surrounded by a forest of modern buildings, and many traditional markets have been replaced by huge department stores.

Right Modern apartment buildings tower over traditional-style houses, in the center of Seoul.

Left Fruit on sale in Namdaemun market, a traditional market in central Seoul. The market is popular with local residents and tourists alike.

Opposite The ancient city of Seoul has been transformed into a modern capital.

Seoul is a center of production and consumption. Many factories and offices are concentrated in the city itself, whereas various service industries are located on the outskirts, in industrial and business areas, or in shopping districts. The shopping districts with their many magnificent department stores contrast with the industrial areas within Seoul. In the busy shopping districts, imported luxury goods are on sale, and there are many restaurants offering American, Japanese, Chinese, and French menus as well as Korean food. However, there is a big gap between the rich and poor areas of Seoul, and the city contains both urban splendor and poverty.

Above *Shoppers crowd into the shopping districts of Seoul on weekends.*

Right *Yung-Man Ahn, office worker*

"City life in Seoul can be very stressful and hard on the nerves; I suppose big cities are always like this. So much rushing around, and so many people. It takes me about one and a half hours to drive to work from where I live on the outskirts of the city. As the city becomes bigger, there are of course more buildings everywhere and fewer areas of open space. I need to escape on the weekend, to walk in the park or the countryside with my children."
—*Yung-Man Ahn, age 35, office worker*

Rural Life and Work

Before the 1960s, South Korea was a typical agricultural country. Since then, the fast growth of a few cities has caused the rural population to move to urban areas. Many parts of rural areas have been swallowed up by industrial expansion. However, agriculture remains important, because rice is still the staple food for South Koreans, and rural areas in South Korea retain their traditional culture.

"In the rush to industrialize, Korean farmers feel left behind. Many farmers have migrated to the industrial centers for other jobs, and farmers rely ever more on foreign technology and imported agricultural products. Farmers are losing the basis of their traditional skills and rural culture. But we know if we adapt, and get the support of good government policies, we can compete even in the world markets." —**Ki Soo Park, age 38, farmer**

Above *A farmer at work in Chinchon, in central South Korea*

Above *The thatched roofs of a traditional South Korean village. Scenes like this are now rare, even in the national parks.*

URBANIZATION SINCE 1960 (thousands)				
	1960	1970	1980	1990
Total population	24,989	31,434	37,449	43,520
Urban	8,947	15,652	25,738	36,013
Rural	16,042	15,782	11,711	7,507
Source: *Economic development and the change of spatial structure in Korea*, D. H. Kim (1992)				

AGRICULTURE

Many South Koreans in rural areas still judge the success of their government by the results of the agricultural harvest. To them, a good harvest means that the government has done well and has been taken care of by their god. A good harvest requires a suitable climate, with the right balance of sunny and rainy days during spring, summer, and autumn. Farmers depend on natural conditions and traditionally believe that good weather is a gift from the gods.

Above A spring festival, when farmers pray for a good harvest, marks the planting of the rice.

Right A farmer in a rural area of central South Korea

Below Gathering the harvest

Although many aspects of South Korean society have become more Westernized, the food culture has not changed dramatically. Rice has always been an important crop. In 1965 rice accounted for 53.7 percent of South Korea's total grain production, and by 1991 it had risen to 86.3 percent.

In addition to producing rice, farmers also grow barley, wheat, fruit, and vegetables. South Korea is famous for fruits such as apples, pears, peaches, mandarin oranges, grapes, and watermelons; its apples and pears, in particular, are well known around the world for their sweet taste and flavor. A vast number of vegetables used for cooking, vegetable oils, and even medicine are also grown. As the rural population, especially of young people, has decreased, farmers have had to rely more on machinery to do the work.

"[In South Korea]… if you walk in the country, you could imagine that the countryside itself is a museum because each landscape has a unique local culture."—from **My Fieldwork Notes of the Cultural Heritage** *by Hong Joon Yu, 1993*

FISHING

Industrialization has also affected fishing regions. Traditional fishing ports and villages have been transformed into huge export ports and industrial areas. As the income of South Koreans has increased, the consumption of fish has also risen.

There are many Japanese restaurants in South Korea that sell fish in a combination of Korean and Japanese styles, usually raw. The fish is fresh and extremely tasty, especially in restaurants near the coast, because the chef cooks the fish in front of the customers. The type of fish available varies among regions because the water temperatures around the Korean peninsula are different along each coastline, supporting different types of fish.

Above An oyster farm. Most South Koreans believe that oysters are good for their health, especially for their eyes.

Right Fishing boats in the small port of Kanghwa, an island off the west coast. Kanghwa is South Korea's fifth largest island.

*"I work in a village that shows what the past is like, with traditional houses and old-fashioned rural scenes: that is why I wear these traditional clothes. Most of the young children from Seoul who come here have never seen anything like it; they are quite shocked. Modern industry in Korea provides new products that make our lives easier and more comfortable—sometimes it's quite hard to keep up as we are going forward so quickly!"—**Yung Ja Roh, worker in traditional craft village**

RURAL LIFE AND FOLK ART

South Korea's countryside is the birthplace of a rich tradition of folk art, which is still preserved in many places, despite the destructive "dark age" of Japanese rule and the Korean War. Music, dancing, and singing are all important traditional art forms that are products of rural life. Just as the South Korean landscape varies from region to region, so each region has its own traditional art form.

Above Yung Ja Roh

Below A nong-ak *(farmers' dance), performed to celebrate a good harvest.*

The Future

A high-tech display at Samsung Electronics. It is likely that South Korea will soon be totally transformed into a high-tech country.

"South Korea has a growth rate which puts Japan and West Germany —not to mention Great Britain—to shame...."

—from The End of the Third World by Nigel Harris (Penguin, 1986)

South Korea is no longer a Third World, or developing, country. It is economically placed between a First World, or advanced, country and a Third World country. It is now trying to become more advanced through heavy investment in high-tech industries. There are two reasons for this. There has been a dramatic increase in the cost of labor since the mid-1980s, so industries are changing from those that require much labor, or "labor-intensive" industries, to those where human labor can be replaced by machinery —"technology-intensive," or "high-tech," industries. The second reason for the high level of investment is to enable South Korea to compete with the United States and Japan in the world market for high-tech goods such as computers, semiconductors, and communication equipment. However, the change to less labor-intensive methods of production has led to sharp conflicts between companies that are trying to reduce their labor forces and unions fighting for the rights of workers.

> *"I lost my full-time job about eight years ago, and because I was too old to retrain I ended up like this. Not everybody benefits from all this change. Still, I'm quite happy because I can get some work. I collect waste paper, boxes, and even cans and sell them back for recycling—it gives me enough money to live."*
> **—Yong Joung Kwon, age 59, unemployed**

THE POVERTY GAP

The rapid economic growth of South Korea has caused an unequal distribution of wealth, both to individuals and to regions of the country. This unequal wealth has led to serious social problems, such as crime and environmental damage, and to extreme conflict among regions. The reduction of this inequality of income, both individually and regionally, is the next step South Korea needs to take in order to secure a stable society.

Above   Yong Joung Kwon, unemployed

A SINGLE KOREA?

The reunification of North and South Korea is very important to people in both countries. However, to do this would mean unifying two very different political systems, the capitalism of the south and the communism of the north. In 1991, the two states did begin to discuss reunification, but each is suspicious of the other. Solving the tension between them is the biggest task facing South and North Koreans.

Left   North Korean delegates (left) meet South Koreans (right) in July 1994.

Glossary

"Asian tigers" Countries in Asia that have experienced fast economic growth since World War II. They are generally called Newly Industrializing Countries (NICs).

Cold war The period of political hostility and tension between capitalist and communist countries that existed from the end of the 1940s until the late 1980s.

Confucianism The teachings of Confucius, a Chinese philosopher (551–479 B.C.).

Democracy Government by representatives of the people, chosen through elections.

Export-oriented economy An economy that depends on exports.

Exports Goods that are sold abroad.

First World country An industrialized and developed country, such as Great Britain, the United States, and Japan.

Free export zones Industrial regions composed of companies producing goods for export. Companies within these zones do not have to pay national taxes.

Gross Domestic Product (GDP) The total value of all goods and services produced within a nation.

Gross National Product (GNP) The total value of all goods and services produced by a nation, including earnings from foreign investments.

Imports Goods that are bought from other countries.

Irrigation A system of pipes and canals, designed to supply water to crops.

Labor-intensive Using many workers.

Military dictatorship Rule by a member or members of the armed forces. The rulers have absolute authority.

Oriental philosophy Philosophy that is concerned with the East, especially Asian ways of understanding the world.

Peninsula A piece of land that is surrounded on three sides by water.

Per capita Latin for "per head," meaning per person.

Precipitation Rain, snow, or sleet falling to the ground.

Primary industries Industries, such as mining, agriculture, and fishing, that produce raw materials.

Secondary industries Industries that turn raw materials into goods; manufacturing industries.

Semiconductors Devices using substances such as silicon, which conduct electricity more effectively as the temperature increases.

State-oriented economy An economy that is controlled by the government.

Technology-intensive Relying heavily on technology rather than on workers.

Tertiary industries Industries, such as transportation or tourism, that provide a service rather than a product.

Third World country An industrializing, developing, or less developed country, mainly in South America, Africa, or Asia.

Further information

Embassy of the Republic of Korea (South Korea), 2370 Massachusetts Avenue NW, Washington, D.C. 20008

Books to read

Farley, Carol. *Korea: Land of the Morning Calm.* Discovering Our Heritage. New York: Dillon Press, 1989.

Lambert, David. *Asia.* Continents. Austin, TX: Raintree Steck-Vaughn, 1996.

Lerner Publications. Department of Geography Staff, ed. *South Korea in Pictures.* Visual Geography. Minneapolis, MN: Lerner Group, 1989.

Nash, Amy. *North Korea.* Let's Visit Places and Peoples in the World. New York: Chelsea House, 1990.

Shepheard, Patricia. *South Korea.* Let's Visit Places and Peoples of the World. New York: Chelsea House, 1988.

Solberg, S. E. *The Land and People of Korea.* Portraits of the Nations. New York: HarperCollins, 1991.

Stein, R. Conrad. *The Korean War: The Forgotten War.* Springfield, NJ: Enslow, 1994.

Index

Page numbers in **bold** refer to illustrations.